PROPHETIC
VOICE RISING

RELEASING THE GIFT

FRED AND SHERRY WHITE

Fountain Gate Publishers
Athens, Georgia USA

Cover art by Fred White.

Find it online in e-book format for digital readers on Amazon.com.

Published by Fountain Gate Publishers, Athens, Georgia USA
www.FountainGatePublishers.com

Unless otherwise indicated, all Scripture quotations are from the New American Standard Bible® by the Lockman Foundation. Other translations specifically noted include Amplified (AMP), Expanded (EXB), New King James Version (NKJV), and New Living Translation (NLT), Style modifications to Scripture quotes are author's preferences.

Printed in the Unites States of America

ISBN: 978-0-9826135-7-3

Dedication

God has connected us to apostles and prophets who have taught us from God's word and have given us opportunities to grow and develop in the apostolic and prophetic ministries. We say thank you to all those who have gone before us and guided our path.

This book is dedicated to Doug and Rita Roberts who give us oversight in the ministry. Their love, support and prayers have meant so much to us. They have taught us by example and allowed us to operate in our gifts and callings. Their training in using the prophetic gift has helped us to grow stronger and wiser in the Lord.

Fred and Sherry White

TABLE OF CONTENTS

PREFACE

We the Authors (Fred and Sherry White) have been married for over 50 years and have served in some form of ministry for over forty years. Although we wrote this book together, the personal stories are written in Sherry's voice, because she is a warring prophetess.

We both had a call of God on our lives from an early age. Preparation for our calling involved submitting to the Lord's authority, studying the word of God and being taught by anointed ministers. The Lord revealed himself to us in many wonderful ways. We have taught our revelation of him in many different venues in this country and elsewhere. We started teaching the word of God in several congregations, our home and low income areas. Then we started a mission for homeless people, prostitutes, alcoholics and drug addicts in our city. We financed the mission and other ministry activities on our own until others came alongside us to help. We minister in various congregations, homes, jails, prisons and drug rehabilitation centers. Jesus heals, delivers and sets the people free in these services. He changes the lives of people wherever he sends us. This book was birthed out of praying together, studying the word of God together and working in the kingdom together.

Purpose of the Book

The prophetic voice plays a crucial role in the kingdom of God. This book can help readers understand the importance of the prophetic voice. It is focused on helping those with a prophetic calling to develop and release the prophetic gift. The prophetic voice is explained by revelation of the Spirit and by practical experiences. This book is filled with kingdom principles and personal experiences to show readers the wonders of Christ in the prophetic voice.

Organization of the Book

The first three chapters introduce prophecy and the prophetic gifts: prophets, seers, prophetic intercessors and prophetic psalmists. Chapter 4 examines the critical role of the spirit man, with emphasis on the spirit of the prophet. Chapter 5 addresses hearing the voice of the Spirit. This chapter is important, because the Spirit does not speak like a man and his words are not heard by natural ears. Chapter 6 examines the nature of those who operate in the prophetic voice. It emphasizes love which encompasses all other fruit of the Spirit. Chapter 7 explains how those with a prophetic calling are empowered to operate in the prophetic voice. Empowerment relates to the Holy Spirit and his anointing.

The next two chapters explain what the prophetic gift does. Chapter 8 examines the gifts of the Spirit, explaining how these gifts relate to the prophetic voice. Chapter 9 identifies the major impacts of the prophetic voice. All of these are important, but some are better known than others. The final chapter of the book (chapter 10) addresses some major conclusions about developing and releasing the spirit man and spreading revival fires. It shows how the concepts developed in this book can be applied by those with a prophetic calling. The Spirit will show how to effectively apply these concepts.

Preparation for Reading the Book

This book contains spiritual truths best understood when the reader's heart and mind are open and properly prepared. Be willing to lay down any preconceived ideas about the prophetic voice which are not pleasing to the Lord. Prayer helps prepare the heart and mind to receive revelation from the Spirit. The better prepared in prayer you are, the more revelation you will gain. Ask the Lord for a fresh revelation on the prophetic voice. Expect a fire to be ignited in your spirit for the Lord, his kingdom and lost souls.

CHAPTER 1
PROPHETIC VOICE INTRODUCED

I have sent seers and prophets into the earth to establish my kingdom and to bring forth my will, says the Lord. They will speak my words only. Just like those crying in the wilderness, "prepare the way of the Lord" they will prepare the way for the manifestation of the sons of God.

Many desire to know things beyond their own thinking without understanding what to do. God is doing a new thing by revealing himself and making known things to come as if the supernatural boundaries between heaven and earth were being redefined. It's his prophetic voice increasing, and all nations will be affected by what he is doing. The purpose of this book is to explain the prophetic voice, so people can understand it and apply it properly. This first chapter introduces the prophetic voice. Special attention is given to prophecy and to the role and operation of the prophet.

The kingdom of God is a prophetic kingdom built on the prophetic foundation. The kingdom is ruled by the prophet-king, Jesus, who sits on the throne of the prophet-king, David. All the prophets from the beginning of time have foretold of this prophet and his kingdom, because the message about Jesus is the true prophecy inspired by the Spirit. Moses foretold of Jesus, "The Lord God will raise up for you a prophet like me from your brethren; to him you shall give heed to everything he says to you (Acts 3:22).

1

Jesus does nothing in his kingdom without the prophetic voice being involved. The prophetic voice is rising to advance this kingdom. When kingdom citizens understand the crucial role of the prophetic voice, they will prophesy, intercede prophetically, worship prophetically and/or operate in the prophetic office, as the Spirit wills.

The prophetic voice plays a crucial role in God's plan to mature the saints. But it has been rejected frequently because of misunderstanding and misuse. Many leaders oppose the prophetic voice, because it might question their motives, doctrines and/or actions. The prophetic gift has been misused by immature prophets who were not equipped to properly use it and were not under authority with supportive relationships. Despite carnal opposition, the prophetic voice is becoming stronger in the earth today. It is time for God's people to understand the prophetic voice and let it take its proper position among the ministry gifts.

The prophetic voice has many components. Prophets speak God's will into the earth. They are the most obvious component of the prophetic voice. Seers could be grouped in with the prophets, but it is useful to recognize seers do not operate like other prophets. Prophetic intercessors and prophetic psalmists play important roles in advancing the kingdom. Through prayer prophetic intercessors prepare the way for God's will to be accomplished. They drive back evil and bring forth the kingdom. Prophetic psalmists sing God's will. They lead the procession for enthroning the king in the hearts of the people. All believers can have a direct role in the prophetic voice, because all can prophesy. Many play an important role in the prophetic voice through their support, help and encouragement, but these are too many to consider thoroughly. Both the gift of prophecy in believers and the office of prophet are discussed below.

Prophecy

Prophecy is inspired by God, not man. It is the expression of divinely inspired thoughts and words. Prophecy is proclaimed when people are led by the Spirit to speak words which come from God (2 Peter 1:21). Prophecy can strengthen, encourage and comfort (1 Corinthians 14:3).

Prophecy is a gift of the Holy Spirit and is given by the Spirit as he chooses. It is full of the energy of God, because it is the heart of the Father being spoken by a person. He pours out his energy and power into that vessel to speak his words into existence. The Father supernaturally endows that person to give his message to the people. When prophecy is given, movement begins in the supernatural realm. This supernatural movement continues as long as the people receive and act on the prophecy. If the prophecy is not acted upon, then movement is halted.

This supernatural movement of the Spirit is illustrated by Elisha's prophecy to a widow. Elisha told the widow to borrow many empty pots from her neighbors and then fill them from her one small pot of oil (2 Kings 4:1–7). Her sons gathered many pots and she miraculously filled them with oil, because her oil multiplied. The oil continued to flow as long as there were empty vessels in which to pour the oil. The oil stopped flowing when there were no more empty vessels. The widow and her sons limited the flow of the Spirit by not gathering more empty vessels.

Every believer can prophesy, but it takes faith to prophesy. People believe they hear a message in the spirit and begin to prophesy out loud. By stepping out in faith they may begin to prophesy without knowing the full message, trusting they hear from God. Believers should prophesy according to the amount of faith they have (Romans 12:6). As a believer's faith increases, he/she would be expected to prophesy more often and in more depth.

Although everyone can prophesy, everyone is not a prophet (1 Corinthians 12:29 and 14:31). Like some things which fly are not birds (e.g. planes and mosquitoes), some people who prophesy are not prophets. Anyone who is called to be a prophet will be able to prophesy.

Prophets

A prophet is called to be a prophet. "Before I formed you in the womb I knew you, and before you were born I consecrated you; I have appointed you a prophet to the nations" (Jeremiah 1:5). The calling of prophets sets them apart from others. Their authority and power is elevated to greater heights than others.

The office of prophet carries a great responsibility, because a prophet speaks for the Lord. The Lord will not allow his words to be polluted by being mixed with carnal thinking. His words are like a pure stream of water. Prophetic words exist and have life when they are spoken. Prophetic words travel through the atmosphere. "He sends forth his command to the earth; his word runs very swiftly" (Psalm 147:15). The words travel, because they are being sent and they have a destination. "He sent his word and healed them" (Psalm 107:20). The centurion who told Jesus to just speak (send) the word had great faith (Matthew 8:5–13). The authority of prophets does not lie in what they do, but it lies in what they speak. The Lord utters his voice before his army: God's words carry authority to move. The prophetic word can be a war cry which means the army is to charge.

The prophetic voice lays out the pattern for the building. The prophetic represents the Father's will. The prophetic sees the invisible and brings those things into this time dimension. For example, the prophet Abraham saw Jesus' day and rejoiced in it (John 8:56). By faith he brought Jesus into his day. The prophetic voice "calls into being things which did not exist" (Romans 4:17). The prophetic voice brings life, increase and comfort and heals the brokenhearted. When the prophet brings comfort and hope, he/she helps establish the hearts of people.

The Lord reveals whatever he does to his prophets. "Surely, the Lord God does nothing unless he reveals his secret counsel to his servants the prophets" (Amos 3:7). A true prophet only speaks the word of God as the Spirit directs. Their motivation is to establish and advance the kingdom of God in the earth.

Prophets are known for making very clear distinctions between right and wrong. They are like skilled surgeons who cut out carnality and bring forth the truth. They are motivated by love but their love may appear to be strange, because they love the people so much they tell them the truth. Jesus was motivated by love when he called the religious leaders poisonous snakes (Matthew 23:33). Prophets who appear to be harsh may be exhibiting great boldness. Each prophet has a unique personality and approach to the prophetic ministry. Such factors as experience, education, relationships and understanding of the gift influence a prophet's ministry. Motivational gifts also influence this ministry. Prophets motivated by mercy may appear to be more lenient than other prophets, because they want to give people an opportunity to change.

Fiery Prophets

The great prophets of all ages have been fiery prophets. God "makes his angels winds and his ministering servants flames of fire" (Hebrews 1:7 AMP). A prophet without the fire of God is not close to God for our God is a consuming fire (Hebrews 12:29). He sets his ministers on fire before sending them out to minister. Fire was in the prophet Jeremiah's mind and heart as if it were shut up in his bones (Jeremiah 20:9 AMP). Elijah called down fire from heaven to consume his enemies (2 Kings 1:9–12). He ascended to heaven in a whirlwind with a chariot of fire and horses of fire (2 Kings 2:11). The Old Testament ended with a prophecy about the spirit of Elijah returning to reconcile the hearts of the fathers and the children (Malachi 4:5–6). God is sending fiery prophets across the land. Fiery prophets change hearts toward God not just minds. A changed heart will affect the mind.

If a person's heart is recreated but his/her mind is not renewed, the person is carnally minded. Carnality relates to those thought patterns which oppose God. Carnality is not washed away; it has to be burned up by the fire of God. Carnality is not destroyed by changing one mind set for another mind set. Justice is served with fire: "in flaming fire taking vengeance on those who do not know God and on those who do not obey the gospel of our Lord Jesus Christ" (2 Thessalonians 1:8 NKJV). Those believers who receive fiery prophets have their thinking changed forever.

PROPHETIC VOICE INTRODUCED

The Prophetic Gift and the Five-fold Ministry

When Jesus vanquished all foes and freed the prisoners, he led a triumphant procession and gave gifts to mankind. He has given these gifts lavishly ever since. These gifts are the five-fold ministry gifts of apostles, prophets, evangelists, pastors and teachers (Ephesians 4:8–11). Jesus had prophesied of another line of apostles and prophets being sent in every generation. "I will send to them prophets and apostles, and some of them they will kill and some they will persecute" (Luke 11:49). All the prophets call for people to obey God. Every generation has to give an account for how it receives the prophetic voice. The religious leaders did not embrace Jesus, who is the truth, nor did they help the people. "You weigh men down with burdens hard to bear, while you yourselves will not even touch the burdens with one of your fingers" (Luke 11:46). When the leaders distort the truth or become insensitive to the needs of the people, they reject the prophets just like those before them. "The blood of all the prophets, shed since the foundation of the world, may be charged against this generation" (Luke 11:50).

Any of the ministry gifts may operate alone in a limited fashion, but they are more effective by operating together through relationships. A prophet who has no relationships with other five-fold ministry gifts is still a prophet but not an effective, five-fold prophet. A five-fold prophet has spiritual relationships with other five-fold ministry gifts, especially apostles. These five-fold ministry gifts equip the saints to do their work (Ephesians 4:12).

Apostles and prophets are the foundation ministry gifts. Jesus is building his church on the foundation of apostles and prophets with himself being the chief cornerstone (Ephesians 2:20). The mystery of God's plan "has now been revealed to his holy apostles and prophets in the Spirit" (Ephesians 3:5). The apostles and prophets know the deep things of the Lord and show them to the body of Christ. They hear the Spirit and flow with the Spirit. Apostles hear on a different frequency than other believers. Prophets see on a deeper level than other believers. Prophets are able to see energy and movement in the supernatural realm and bring into focus what God is doing. They see the various facets of what God is doing and how things connect. Apostles and prophets have an uncommon commitment to the commons, which are the things shared by many.

The apostles go into new territory and establish God's kingdom in that territory. The prophets give direction. The prophet cannot override the apostle, because the apostle first brings the authority and then the prophet comes in with the direction. Those two ministry gifts have been missing in the body of Christ. The body has had neither authority nor direction. The same thing has happened in the body of Christ which happened in the Garden of Eden—the emergence of man and his thinking. When Jesus came on the scene, he brought back to the earth the will of the Father, and in the garden he submitted to the Father.

Prophets and Seers

A seer is a prophet with a unique ability to see what God is doing. A seer is another name for a prophet. "Formerly in Israel, when a man went to inquire of God, he used to say, "Come, and let us go to the seer"; for he who is called a prophet now was formerly called a seer" (1 Samuel 9:9). A seer is a prophet who sees visions and dreams. In addition to the ability to see visions, a seer has insight into what is meant by these visions.

Both prophets and seers are identified in the word of God. The acts of Solomon are written in the records of Nathan the prophet, in the prophecy of Ahijah, and in the visions of Iddo the seer (2 Chronicles 9:29). Nathan apparently heard God's voice, while Iddo saw what God was doing through visions. The prophet Jeremiah was a seer, because God frequently showed him visions and asked him what he saw (Jeremiah 1:11–13). God gave Jeremiah understanding about the meaning of visions (Jeremiah 1:14–18).

Many people had visions in the New Testament. Zacharias saw a vision in the temple about his future son, John (Luke 1:22). The Lord spoke in a vision to Aninias about Saul, and he spoke in a vision to Saul about Aninias (Acts 9:10–12). The Lord spoke in a vision to Cornelius about Simon Peter, and then he spoke in a vision to Simon Peter concerning the ministry to Cornelius (Acts 10:3–17).

There will always be prophets who see visions. Joel prophesied about the outpouring of the Spirit in which "your young men will see visions and your old men will dream dreams" (Joel 2:28). This prophecy is happening now. God gave dreams and visions to his leaders like Abraham, Joseph, Joshua, Daniel, Paul and Peter to empower them for the work of the kingdom. Joseph dreamed dreams and interpreted dreams. As a young boy, he dreamed his brothers would bow down to him (Genesis 37:5–11). His brothers hated him and sold him into slavery in Egypt. Later, Joseph was put in prison where he interpreted dreams. He interpreted two dreams for Pharaoh (Genesis 41:14–32). Pharaoh promoted Joseph to a position of great authority. His brothers had to come to Egypt to get grain because of the famine in the land. Joseph was in charge of the grain, and his brothers had to bow down to him to get what they needed (Genesis 42:6). Joseph saw the fulfillment of his dreams.

God communicated with his people and gave them directions through dreams and visions. He is still doing the same thing today. Dreams and visions from God activate faith inside believers causing them to go beyond their own thinking and their own abilities. Visions and dreams can always be confirmed through the Spirit of God and his word. Dreams or visions which cause stress, fear, anxiety or doubt are not from the Lord and should be discarded from the mind.

Dreams and visions empower believers to go forward into their purpose and destiny. They are a form of communication between God and man. God gives instruction, direction and even warnings through dreams and visions. Prophetic dreams and visions often relate to the body of Christ and the plan of God for his body.

Personal Stories about Dreams and Visions

The Lord gives me (Sherry) dreams and visions, and many people call me to interpret their dreams. There are times when I have had open visions which are similar to watching a TV screen. Some are in color, but all are vivid. One vision occurred while I was preparing for the day. I looked in my bathroom mirror and there in the mirror was a black man kneeling in front of the Lord. He asked the Lord, "What is required of me?" The Lord spoke back to him and said, "One thing is required of you and that is to love." Then the vision left. I pondered what I had seen and shared it with another prayer warrior. She began to tremble and related the vision to William Seymour from the Azusa Street revival. She had read a book about William Seymour which describes an incident in which he knelt before the Lord and asked what was required of him, and the Lord replied he only had to love. It was a significant moment in my life, because I felt the Lord was saying the same thing to me: love all people.

Another vision came as I was driving to a meeting in another state. I saw myself driving a black Mercedes with camel interior. I got excited, because in the natural I was driving an inexpensive minivan. I began to proclaim I was driving a black Mercedes with camel interior. Three years later I was driving a new, black Mercedes with camel interior, and I drove that wonderful car for 11 years. It was God's car, and it was used for his work. I was reminded of the scripture in Genesis where Abraham was told to take his son to the mountain to sacrifice him, but Abraham said the Lord will provide himself a sacrifice. God provided a sacrifice for Abraham, and he provided a black Mercedes for me. It was his car, but I drove it.

Conclusions

The prophetic voice speaks for the Lord and plays a crucial role in God's plan to mature the saints. When believers understand and receive the prophetic voice it brings repentance for sin and direction to the body of Christ. When those called as prophets understand and activate the gift, they become effective spiritual leaders. If the prophetic voice is rejected, the body of Christ suffers with carnality. If it is received, the saints are matured and equipped to do their work. Every generation will answer for whether the prophetic voice is received. It is time for the prophetic voice to rise again and bring repentance and revival to the body of Christ.

CHAPTER 2
PROPHETIC INTERCESSION

Many are in desperation and tribulation. I have called those who would hear my voice to stand in the gap for my people, says the Lord of hosts. As they intercede, I will hear their cries and deliver my people.

God's kingdom is destined to increase without limits. "There will be no end to the increase of his government or of peace" (Isaiah 9:7). This increase is made possible by prayer and prophetic intercession. Prophetic intercessors are those prophets and prayer warriors ordained to drive back the forces of darkness and advance the kingdom through spiritual warfare. Prayer and intercession are needed to release the prophetic voice for the kingdom to advance. The Lord is calling intercessors to an active prayer life to bring them closer to him and prepare their hearts for spiritual battles. This chapter examines the purpose and impact of prophetic intercession.

Intercessors drive back evil forces and gross darkness for God's will to come forth. Lifting up petitions to God is not prophetic intercession. Without intercession leaders fail, carnality abounds and the lost perish. Strategic intercession is needed for every aspect of ministry. Intercession focused on one aspect of ministry such as salvation does not necessarily support other areas such as the promotion of spiritual growth. No area of ministry can be neglected by prayer warriors and prophetic intercessors without adverse consequences.

Preparing for a Life of Intercession

A call to intercession leads to a path traveled by only a few and understood by even fewer. Intercession is not like an office job with limited and convenient hours of work, because intercessors are always on call. Their path is one of faith, intimacy with the Lord and prayer. The Lord desires to share his thoughts and plans with them.

To remain on the path intercessors must watch and stay alert. They watch and pray so they do not get involved with man's thinking and plans. "No soldier in active service entangles himself in the affairs of everyday life" (2 Timothy 2:4). Intercessors stay girded up for the battle. Intercessors play key roles in God's army, but without an active prayer life they are ineffective soldiers.

Intercessors are like eagles soaring above the situations in the spiritual realm. They are fearless and fiercer than other believers who are not called to intercession. They are called by God for such a time as this. By watching and praying, they will see the Lord coming to lead his troops into victory. The enemy is moving upon the church with great fierceness. His plan has already been activated. "Be of sober spirit, be on the alert. Your adversary, the devil, prowls around like a roaring lion, seeking someone to devour" (1 Peter 5:8). Intercessors are quick to respond to the Father's will, as well as any enemy movement.

Prayer keeps people humble so they can receive from the Lord. If they continue to watch and pray, God's plan becomes fully known. Prayer releases Gods perfect will into the earth and gives him freedom to move. As believers humble themselves and pray, the petitions they ask for are granted.

Prayer Stops the Adversary

The armor of God is not natural armor to fight natural adversaries. It is prayer armor to war against rulers of darkness and spiritual wickedness (Ephesians 6:10–18). The adversaries are not people but evil spirit beings. "With all prayer and petition pray at all times in the spirit, and with this in view, be on the alert with all perseverance and petition for all the saints" (Ephesians 6:18).

In 1992, I had some health problems and was tested by physicians. We prayed and stood for healing in faith. After several tests, three physicians agreed I had cancer and might not live six months. Our faith in the healing power of Jesus remained strong. One night the Spirit gave me a scripture for my situation: "I will not die, but live, and tell of the works of the Lord" (Psalm 118:17). The Lord healed me, and even the physician recognized my miracle. I am thankful for my healing. I continue to be free from cancer and serve the Lord.

Prophecy Stops the Adversary

It is important for believers to hear from the Lord themselves and to be around others who hear from the Lord and operate in the gifts of the Spirit. Prophecy can be used to stop the work of the adversary. "This command I entrust to you, Timothy, my son, in accordance with the prophecies previously made concerning you, that by them you fight the good fight" (1 Timothy 1:18). We have had to fight and believe the Lord to heal and deliver a member of our family who had an issue with drug abuse. Several prophets of God in different places gave us a word of comfort and exhortation concerning this person. They all said he would be delivered from drugs and would serve the Lord. As situations concerning the drug issues arose, these prophetic words would be brought back to our remembrance by the Holy Spirit. Our strength would return, and we would be able to stand.

Intercession

Intercession brings forth Christ in the people. Paul travailed in birth for the people to be born again and then travailed a second time for Christ to be manifested in their lives (Galatians 4:19). Prophetic intercessors stand in the gap between good and evil, driving back evil and bringing forth God's kingdom.

Intercessors labor to birth God's perfect will into the earth. Their travail in the spirit will result in lives being changed and a newness to come forth (1 Thessalonians 2:9). Jeremiah was a weeping prophet. He cried out for the people of God. Rachel cried out for the children (Matthew 2:18). The Spirit of God takes hold with intercessors to push through situations in their lives and to birth God's perfect will (Romans 8:26). Travailing in the spirit is a deep level of intercession. It takes intercessors into the middle of situations and lets them prophesy God's perfect will.

Intercession is the manifestation of Jesus being head. When the body of Christ stands up in its rightful position under the headship of Jesus, there will be prayer offered continually. Jesus ever lives to intercede (Hebrews 7:25). Without intercession, the body will not increase. Intercession, which comes straight out of the love of God, pours out his love on the body.

Carnality hinders efforts to pray and answers to prayer. Some carnal people pray for the rain of the Spirit to fall on them, but their prayers seem to be unanswered. It takes the prophetic voice to move the people from the carnal realm to the spiritual where they can experience the rain of the Spirit. The rain of the Spirit is God pouring out his love on a people or specific event. Some call it revival, because it brings a renewal and a refreshing concerning spiritual life.

The Lord's house, his church, is built on Jesus, the revealed word of God. His house is a house of prayer. For all who seek the Lord will find he is there, ever present and all knowing. Those who hunger and thirst for the Lord will be filled and their cup will overflow.

Prophetic intercessors stand against sin, and pray for repentant hearts. Without repentance there is no cleansing. They will not hold back. The Lord has prepared the prophetic voice for this hour. The effective prayer of a righteous person will produce an overflowing of the Spirit (James 5:16). As the prophetic voice sounds, people will turn to the Lord, but it is only the beginning.

Personal Stories on Prophetic Intercession

There are times when intercession comes upon me, and I begin to pray. Sometimes I know what I am praying for and sometimes I don't. One day, while Fred was in another state, the spirit of intercession came upon me, and I prayed fervently for about thirty minutes. I knew it was for him. At the time I was praying for him, he came through a serious car accident safely. No one in either car was injured. God was warring for him through me and saved his life.

The spirit of intercession came on me to pray for the people in Africa. I prayed for Africa for nine years before an opportunity arose for me to minister in Africa. The Lord provided all the finances needed for the ministry trip. He healed the sick and performed miracles as I ministered to the people of Africa.

Conclusions

Intercession is needed for those who are lost to be saved and for believers to be matured. Prophetic intercession is the highest form of intercession, because it prays the Father's perfect will to bring forth his kingdom. Prophetic intercessors can lead others in prayer if they are trained in the prophetic move of the Spirit, but they are stifled in carnal prayer meetings. Prophetic intercessors are being called to increase intercession in order to strengthen the body of Christ.

CHAPTER 3
PROPHETIC PSALMS

Let the earth rejoice and give praise unto my name, says the Lord. This is the time to bring forth the fruit of your mouth and rejoice in my presence. Let your mouth open wide and I will fill it to overflowing. The earth will spring forth and the deserts will bloom. My Spirit will pour out and water the earth. No longer will it be barren.

Prophetic psalmists hear the sounds of heaven and sing the new song. This is the new song called for in the psalms. "Sing to the Lord a new song; sing to the Lord, all the earth" (Psalm 96:1). The new song is a prophetic psalm which comes out of the depths of the heart. "The mouth speaks out of that which fills the heart" (Matthew 12:34). The heart has supernatural rhythms, and the new song comes out of the rhythms of the heart. This chapter examines the role of the prophetic psalmist.

Prophetic psalmists usher in the glory, which is the very presence of the Lord. They help enthrone the Lord in the hearts of the people and bring forth his glory. "May the whole earth be filled with his glory" (Psalm 72:19). The prophetic psalm fills the hearts of the people with his glory. It is powerful when it is sung.

Psalmist Anointing

The prophet-king David is the foremost prophetic psalmist. There was no mention of David in the word of God until Samuel came to anoint him. Samuel took the horn of oil and anointed David and the Spirit of the Lord came mightily upon him from that day forward (1 Samuel 16:13). Whatever David was going through, he sang songs about it. When he was far away from the Lord he sang songs, and when he was close to the Lord he sang songs. David had a song for everything. When he was sorrowful or rejoicing he had a song. When he needed shelter he sang a song, because his heart was connected to God's heart. God said, "I have found David the son of Jesse, a man after my heart, who will do all my will" (Acts 13:22). The kingdom was established in David's heart before he established it on the earth. Prophetic songs for the Lord arose from his heart. He played a harp and sang these songs, which became the best known prophetic psalms. He walked in the spiritual realm and received revelation of the Lord before his time. David caught the sounds of heaven. His ear was tuned to God's frequency, and he caught the tunes and played them on his harp. Those who can hear the rhythms to sing a prophetic psalm are like David.

One day Fred had an attack on his body while at work. His staff called me to say he might be having a heart attack. I drove to his office and got him into the car, but he did not want to go to the hospital. He felt like his head was exploding. He could not get comfortable in any position and could never be still. He walked, sat on a chair, and lay on our couch, but nothing helped. As he lay on the couch, our daughter, who is an anointed psalmist, began to play her guitar and sing over him. The evil spirit departed from Fred. He did not gradually mend or receive a healing, but he received an immediate deliverance. This experience was just like the one which happened to Saul when David played his harp (1 Samuel 16:23). Evil spirits departed from Saul and from Fred.

The Spirit's anointing is given for ministry to the people. It abides on God's word and flows like a river out from his throne. It flows through and by the Spirit. The anointing is God's ultimate power energized or activated in psalmists. The anointing within psalmists who are willing to be used by God confirms the truth. Without the anointing, God's people will doubt the truth but believe lies. Speaking the anointed word destroys the works of the devil and sets people free.

The anointing is the vehicle that carries the secrets of God. It's like a spaceship which comes to earth, makes a deposit and then leaves. The anointing operates in the supernatural realm, rather than the natural realm. The anointing guides psalmists to the heart of God.

Psalmists can walk in a greater anointing by keeping their hearts pure and staying in the presence of the Lord. The anointing is God's power that flows from his heart. Only those with a pure heart and clean hands can ascend to the mountain of God and receive from him (Psalm 24:3–5).

Like kings were anointed at their coronation, Jesus was anointed with joy. "Your God has anointed you, pouring out the oil of joy on you more than on anyone else" (Hebrews 1:9 NLT). His anointing of joy produced a sweet fragrance which attracted people to him. It is called the fragrance of the Anointed One (2 Corinthians 2:15). The anointing brings joy and the strength of the Lord. "The joy of the Lord is your strength" (Nehemiah 8:10). Joy enabled Jesus to endure great suffering on the cross. Just as Jesus was anointed with joy, he anoints psalmists with his joy before sending them out as his ambassadors. Jesus said, "I have told you these things so that you can have the same joy I have" (John 15:11 EXB). Psalmists carry the fragrance of the anointing as they spread the knowledge of Christ.

Anointed to bring forth Life

The Lord God walked and talked with Adam and Eve in the cool of the evening. He commanded them to be fruitful and multiply (Genesis 1:28). He revealed himself to them so they might reproduce him. Like all believers, psalmists are predestined to be conformed to the image of his Son (Romans 8:29). However, the carnal mind does not understand what God meant when he said to be fruitful and multiply. Adam and Eve ate fruit of the forbidden tree and reproduced themselves. A natural man reproduces himself, and a religious man reproduces himself. But a son of God reproduces his Father. The anointing is given to reproduce spiritual life. The anointing brought life to Jesus and raised him from the dead. The anointing available to psalmists and energized within them is the same power God used to raise Christ from the dead (Ephesians 1:19–20 and 3:20).

Price of the Anointing

As shown in the parable of the ten virgins, there is a price to be paid for the precious oil (Matthew 25:1–9). Oil in the parable symbolizes the anointing. The virgins who wanted more oil to fuel their light were instructed to go where oil was bought and sold and pay the price for their own oil. Virgins can be those who are born again with their innocence restored by Jesus. Even though they were virgins, they wanted more of the precious oil. For more anointing, psalmists pay the price of sacrificing their will to do the Father's will. Jesus said, "If anyone wishes to come after me, he must deny himself, and take up his cross and follow me" (Matthew

16:24). Kathryn Kuhlman had a great anointing for healing the sick and miracles, ministering to great multitudes. When asked about the anointing, she said it cost her everything.

True Worship

The spirit of the prophet, which is crated for intimate fellowship with the Father, becomes fully engaged in true worship. "God is spirit, and those who worship him must worship in spirit and truth" (John 4:24). Worship is a place in the spirit behind the veil in the presence of the Lord where worshipers can go. It's a place of being consumed by the presence of the Lord. Fleshly desires, fears and anxieties are burned up in the presence of the Lord for he is a consuming fire (Hebrews 12:29). A worshiper's perspective changes as the Lord is magnified over his/her worldly situations. Temporal things become less significant than previously thought when the worshiper faces eternity in the presence of the Lord.

One way to help understand worship is to compare it with praise. Many people think fast, loud songs are praise, while slow, soft songs are worship. Worship is not a song at all but an encounter with the Lord. Songs may facilitate entering into the worship experience, but they are not to be confused with true worship. Worship is a higher place than praise. Carnal people can praise the Lord, but it takes a spiritual person to worship him in spirit and truth.

Two things are critical for entering worship: faith and recognition of the finished work of the cross. True worship comes out of faith. A mother came to Jesus and asked for her daughter to be delivered from a demon (Matthew 15:22–28). Nothing happened until she humbled herself and worshiped Jesus. She demonstrated humility when she was willing to accept the crumbs

23

from the Master's table. When she worshiped Jesus, he acknowledged her great faith and the daughter's deliverance from an evil spirit. Activating faith in worship brings healing, deliverance and victory.

True worship is focused on the finished work of the cross. Any worship that is not based on the finished work of the cross is a fraud and an insult to the crucifixion and resurrection of Jesus Christ. It's the finished work of the cross which gives worshipers access to the presence of the Lord (Romans 5:1–2). Worshipers are continually worshiping the Lamb of God around the throne of God (Revelation 7:10–13). The Lamb of God is the temple and the light of the heavenly Jerusalem (Revelation 21:22–23). True worshipers ascribe all power to the resurrected Savior and none to any enemy of the cross. They declare the precious name of Jesus, which is above every other name. The precious blood of Jesus Christ redeemed us (1 Peter 1:18–19). Worshipers plead the shed blood of Jesus over their lives and situations. His blood is incorruptible and able to cleanse, sanctify, heal, and deliver. Worship becomes more effective by focusing on Jesus and those things which he accomplished at the cross.

Worshipers can expect powerful moves of the Holy Spirit in worship when they deny all selfish interests and fully commit to doing the Lord's will. Then each encounter with the Lord will bring changes in the life of a true worshiper. If nothing happens or changes as a result of worshiping the Lord, then something in the worship experience is not right. Life changing experiences come out of true worship.

Personal Stories of a Prophetic Psalmist

I remember the day I was reading about the Easter story and the woman who saw Jesus in the garden and supposed him to be the gardener. His appearance had changed. She was crying, and Jesus said to her, "Woman, why do you weep?" She replied they had taken her lord, and she did not know where he was. Then Jesus spoke her name, and she knew it was Jesus. The Spirit began to give me a song for the body of Christ. He said the weeping and mourning time was over and he wanted his body to rejoice, because he was alive and alive forevermore. The song, Woman Don't You Weep, was birthed. In the prophetic song he tells the woman not to weep anymore, because he is alive and has conquered death. The grave could not hold him and he arose to live forevermore with the Father. He tells her to rejoice for the victory belongs to hers. This song has been an encouragement to me and to others not only at Easter, but any time it is sung. On that day the river of God was flowing straight from his throne through me. There was another memorable time when the prophetic began to flow in song. Another prayer warrior and I were praying for the body of Christ, and the Spirit of the Lord came upon us, and we began to prophesy in song. The song was about gathering together and singing a new song unto the Lord. It was about unity and laying down all division. One verse of the song tells about looking for the signs of his coming, like the fruit on the fig tree. While singing the new song, we knew we were operating as prophetic psalmists. A prophetic song will always glorify the Father and bring honor to him.

Conclusions

Prophetic psalmists can produce a sweet fragrance of the Lord which draws people into his presence. The proper application of such gifts in worship leadership can be very beneficial. A prophetic psalmist may lead other musicians and singers who are trained to flow with the Spirit, but a prophetic psalmist will never fit well with a carnal praise group who wants to take advantage of natural talent.

CHAPTER 4
SPIRIT OF THE PROPHET

Surely, the spirit of the prophet is alive and connected to my Holy Spirit, says the Lord. I speak and the prophet's spirit hears what I say. My prophets proclaim and declare my words out of their spirits. They are quick to obey my will and my commands. Through their spirits flow my life and my power.

While the spirit man for a typical believer can rise up to fight like a soldier in the militia, the spirit of the prophet is created for strategic warfare. The spirit of the prophet is a fierce warrior wielding the two-edged prophetic sword of the Spirit. It is submitted to the prophet like a warrior is subject to the commander (1 Corinthians 14:32). The spirit of the prophet relates to the prophet, the seer, the prophetic intercessor and the prophetic psalmist. The prophet and the seer are strategists in battle, because they see the battle from God's perspective and direct his forces. The prophetic words spoken by the prophet and the seer establish the kingdom of God in the hearts of the people. The prophetic intercessor advances the kingdom with conquests over evil. The prophetic psalmist fights through unbelief and carnal distractions to establish true worship and enthrone King Jesus in the hearts of the people. This chapter examines how to bring forth the spirit of the prophet as a mighty warrior.

Introducing Spirit of the Prophet

The spirit of the prophet is like fine crystal, transparent to the Lord. Crystal makes a beautiful sound. Crystal has to be handled very carefully, because it is fragile and subject to scratches and cracks. It takes very hot fire to mend broken crystal, as well as a broken spirit. If there is a film on crystal, it is cloudy and hard to see through. Doctrines and traditions of men make the spirit of the prophet dark like cloudy crystal. It has to be washed with the pure water of the word.

While the soul and body of the prophet are connected to the natural realm, the spirit of the prophet is connected to the supernatural realm. The prophet is joined to the Lord in the supernatural realm through his/her spirit. "The spirit of man is the lamp of the Lord" (Proverbs 20:27). Just as the Lord is spirit, so the prophet is spirit. "The one who joins himself to the Lord is one spirit with him" (1 Corinthians 6:17). Prophecy comes through the spirit of the prophet, so it has nothing to do with the carnal mind. The prophet operates as the Holy Spirit determines. When the spirit of the prophet prays, sings or prophesies, the mind is inactive. Paul wrote when my spirit prays by the Holy Spirit within me, my mind is unproductive (1 Corinthians 14:14 AMP). Prophecy bypasses the mind.

The prophet sees many things but only speaks those things the Father wants done. For example, the prophet speaks unity in the midst of division. The enemy wants the prophet to speak what is being seen in the natural realm, but changes occur in the supernatural realm. Prophecy speaks to the spirit man, and when it is received there will be life-changing results.

Elders laid hands on Timothy and imparted a spiritual gift to him. He was instructed to stir up the gift. "Kindle afresh the gift of God which is in you through the laying on of my hands (2 Timothy 1:6). "Do not neglect the spiritual gift within you, which was bestowed on you through prophetic utterance with the laying on of hands by the presbytery" (1 Timothy 4:14). Spiritual elders who lay hands on ministers to ordain them and operate with prophetic utterances can impart spiritual gifts such as prophecy and ministry gifts such as the prophet. Each person called to be a prophet needs to find God's ordained relationships with spiritual elders who can impart these gifts to them. Once the gift of prophecy and the prophetic ministry gift have been imparted to a prophet, they both reside within the spirit of the prophet. It is the responsibility of each prophet to keep these gifts active and blazing hot.

Uniting the Spirit and Soul of the Prophet

Before salvation, the spirit man is dormant and the soul, which consists of the mind, will and emotions, is fleshly or natural. The soul was hostile towards God and will continue to be the same way until the spirit is recreated and the mind renewed to the word of God.

After salvation the spirit of the prophet must be nurtured and developed through the word of God and by his Spirit. Without spiritual food and development, the spirit of the prophet remains malnourished, impoverished and imprisoned. The word of God is food for spiritual growth (1 Peter 2:2). Prayer is needed to develop the spirit of the prophet. Being in the presence of God through his word and prayer is critical for developing the spirit of the prophet.

After the spirit of the prophet is recreated the prophet's soul should be renewed and saved (Ephesians 4:23–24). It takes the anointed word of God to renew the mind and save the soul (James 1:21). Until the mind is renewed, the prophet experiences a struggle between the recreated spirit and the old nature or flesh which wants to control the spirit of the prophet (Galatians 5:17). When the flesh rules the spirit of the prophet, the result is carnality. The carnal mind is hostile towards God (Romans 8:7). Prophesying in the flesh is dangerous. It can cause the wrong message to be conveyed. God uses a natural vessel but speaks a spiritual message. When the mind is renewed so the spirit of the prophet rules the flesh there will be oneness in spirit and soul, and the correct message will be given.

The Lord gave me the ability to look inside a person to see the condition of the spirit man or the spirit of the prophet. A malnourished spirit has a large head and a small body. A well-developed spirit looks very much like a human being. The spirit can grow larger than the body in which it resides, because it exists in another realm without physical constraints. He also has given me the ability to look inside of a person physically like an x-ray machine. Then I know exactly what needs to be corrected and healed. I see hearts very clearly and know if arteries need to be cleaned out to prevent heart attacks. This spiritual ability has been extremely helpful when he is healing or performing miracles.

Divine Fellowship

Who really knows the spirit of a prophet? There are a few important things known about the spirit of the prophet. First, the spirit yearns for heavenly things rather than earthly or mundane things. The spirit of the prophet will seek "the things above, where Christ is, seated at the right hand of God" (Colossians 3:1–2). The spirit of the prophet yearns for fellowship with the Lord.

Second, the spirit of the prophet must be liberated to fulfill purpose and destiny. It takes the Holy Spirit to free the spirit of the prophet. "Now the Lord is the Spirit, and where the Spirit of the Lord is, there is liberty" (2 Corinthians 3:17). The more a prophet communes with the Holy Spirit the freer the spirit of the prophet becomes. Considering the resurrection of Lazarus from the dead helps explain the concept of freeing the spirit man (John 11:41–44). After Jesus called Lazarus from death to life, he still had to be loosed from his grave clothes. Likewise, those called to be a prophet still have to be loosed from all fleshly bondage. Loose the spirit of the prophet and let him go free.

Third, the spirit's general purpose is to yield fruit for the Lord. "The fruit of the Spirit is love, joy, peace, patience, kindness, goodness, faithfulness, gentleness, self-control" (Galatians 5:22–23). When prophets catch hold of what the spirit of the prophet says their mind becomes renewed and fruitful.

Prayer

An effective prayer life is needed to have a fully developed prophetic spirit. The intellectual or carnal mind cannot know what should be prayed in order to bring forth the fullness of the spirit of the prophet. "We do not know what prayer to offer nor how to offer it worthily" (Romans 8:26 AMP). Prophets cannot have the intellectual knowledge concerning how to pray or for what to pray in order to liberate the spirit of the prophet. The spirit of the prophet hungers for things the intellectual mind cannot understand. In particular, the spirit of the prophet can have an understanding of a prophet's purpose and destiny which the carnal mind cannot comprehend. "For who among men knows the thoughts of a man except the spirit of the man which is in him" (1 Corinthians 2:11)? Both the development and release of the spirit of the prophet are important for purpose and destiny to be fulfilled.

Praying in the spirit each day can bring what the spirit man needs for the day. When prophets are filled with the Holy Spirit, they are able to pray in the spirit in order to release their spirits. The spirit man has a mind to pray. "If I pray in a tongue, my spirit prays, but my mind is unfruitful." (1 Corinthians 14:14). Under the guidance of the Holy Spirit, the spirit of the prophet can pray the perfect will of God (Romans 12:1–2). The spirit of the prophet sings the high praises to the Lord (Psalm 149:6). The limitations of the intellectual mind are overcome by praying in the spirit and singing in the spirit.

Fire in the Spirit of the Prophet

The fire of God burns in the spirit of the prophet, not in the flesh. The Lord is like a refiner's fire (Malachi 3:2). He abides in the believer's spirit man and the prophet's spirit. "We are the temple of the living God" (2 Corinthians 6:16). He prepares his prophets with fire to destroy evil and help others (Psalm 104:4). People in the world are searching for those who are burning with flaming fire, because they have already gone through the fire themselves.

The fire will test people's faith. The thing being tested is what they believe. The fire reveals what is inside people, even what they do not know themselves. It burns up what is not of God and begins to mold and shape people so they can be conformed to the image of Christ.

Fire on the inside of a prophet is manifested as the Lord's boldness. A boldness arose in Paul to fulfill the plan and purpose God had for him (Acts 13:46). God knew Paul needed the boldness to face adversaries and persecution. It was no longer Paul's natural boldness but the holy boldness which kept him doing God's will and proclaiming the gospel of the kingdom.

Word of Fire

The word of the Lord is fire. "'Is not my word like fire?' declares the Lord" (Jeremiah 23:29). Out of his mouth comes a flaming sword. When the prophet cried to the Lord for help the earth shook, "because he was angry; smoke went up out of his nostrils, and fire from his mouth devoured" (Psalm 18:7–8). His fire will again destroy wickedness.

Those with an intellectual understanding of the word of God have no fire in their spirits. The prophets who are filled with God's word are filled with his fire. "Behold, I am making my words in your mouth fire and this people wood, and it will consume them" (Jeremiah 5:14). When Jesus spoke to the disciples a fire burned within them. "Were not our hearts burning within us while he was speaking to us on the road, while he was explaining the scriptures to us?" (Luke 24:32).

If the people are fed only the milk of the word, their spirits become like cloudy glass covered with a milky white film. It is difficult to see through cloudy glass with a milky film over it. A person sees God's promises and the things he is doing through his/her spirit man, so the spirit man needs to be clear. Also, the spirit man needs to be healthy and sound. Many people have been wounded or their hearts have been broken, so their spirits have been scratched and cracked. "The spirit of a man can endure his sickness, but as for a broken spirit who can bear it?" (Proverbs 18:14) It takes the fire and the anointing to restore broken vessels, so they can receive God's promises. When the fire of God comes out of a prophet's mouth, the wounded spirits are restored.

Love is the fuel which burns the fire. Faith is energized by love. "Only faith activated and energized and expressed and working through love" counts for anything (Galatians 5:6 AMP). Some who have lost their love for God and people have lost the fire. Without love there is no fire. "Because lawlessness is increased, most people's love will grow cold" (Matthew 24:12).

The spirit of the prophet can be partially or completely filled with fire, two limited forms of fire. The prophet would be in control of both of those forms of fire. There is also an overflowing of fire which is beyond the control of the prophet. In this case the spirit of the prophet would be filled unto overflowing with the fire and immersed in the fire. Jesus Christ is the one who baptizes or immerses people in the fire. John the Baptist declared, "I baptize you with water; but one is coming who is mightier than I, and I am not fit to untie the thong of his sandals; he will baptize you with the Holy Spirit and fire" (Luke 3:16).

Prayers of Fire

Prophets can pray to be filled with God's fire and pray for others to be set on fire. When prophets are filled with God's fire, their words are burning with fire. Some prayers are filled with the fire of the Spirit. "The effective, fervent prayer of a righteous man avails much" (James 5:16 NKJV).

The prophets of old prayed for fire from heaven. Let the god of this nation be the god who answers by fire. This cry came from the heart of Elijah in the midst of a perverse and crooked generation. "You call on the name of your god, and I will call on the name of the Lord, and the god who answers by fire, he is God" (1 Kings 18:24). Let it also be the heart's cry of those serving the Lord.

Personal Story on Fire of God

I remember several years ago when the Lord gave me a vision. I was in the middle of a huge fire but not being consumed. I went to my pastor at the time and asked him what this vision meant. Did it mean I was about to go through tribulation? I will never forget his answer. He said this vision was about being in the very center of God's will and in his presence. God put me there, and nothing could hurt me nor hinder me. I have felt the fire of God in my hands especially praying over people with any cancer. My hands get very hot and red. God's fire burns out all sickness and disease. One woman came up in a service and told me she had breast cancer and asked me to pray for her. I did, and she said immediately she began to feel fire go into the area where there was a mass. She went back to the doctor, and they found no mass. God's fire had burned it up. Praise the Lord forever for his fire.

Conclusions

The spirit of the prophet responsive to the Holy Spirit is God's true prophet, not the outer man, intellect or personality. The prophetic voice has nothing to do with the carnal realm. When the spirit of the prophet is recognized as the true prophet, the prophetic voice sounds loud and clear. The Lord is sending prophets to rekindle fire in the people for his prophets are burning flames of fire. They will go where he sends them. The fire will burn in front of them. As the fire burns, the enemy cannot stand before them. The heathen will come to the light of their fire.

CHAPTER 5
HEARING THE SPIRIT'S VOICE

Let the church of the living God hear my voice. This is the time to lend your spiritual ear to hear what the Spirit would say during these perilous times. I will speak to my church about my will and about my plan. Surely, I do nothing unless I first reveal it to my prophets.

God's prophets are sensitive to the voice of his Spirit. They hear what the Spirit is saying and communicate his message to others through prophetic words. Their prophetic words express what they hear in the spirit and how they hear it. The tone of their message reflects the heavenly tone such as anger, joy or sorrow. A weighty message given frivolously would not be a true reflection of what was being conveyed from heaven. Their words become the voice of the Lord on the earth. It takes a close personal relationship with the Spirit for a prophet to consistently hear his voice and express what he is saying and how he wants people to hear his message. This chapter examines how anyone hears the voice of the Spirit. It will help prophets as well as others tune their spiritual ears to the supernatural realm.

When two people are talking, the words spoken by one person vibrate as sound waves through the air producing energy and are heard by a second person. The person speaking would be the source of the sound; air would be the conductor through which sound travels; and the person hearing the words would be the receiver. Sound cannot travel through a vacuum. Many do not hear the Lord speaking through his Spirit, because they expect him to speak like a man. But he is a spirit and speaks in ways which are mysterious to the carnal mind. The source, conductor and receivers for the Spirit's words make them far different from man's words. These three elements of speech in the supernatural realm are discussed below.

Source and Nature of the Spirit's Words

The Spirit is the breath and the wind of God. All scripture is God-breathed (2 Timothy 3:16 NIV). His words move on the wind and can be called wind words. "Listen to the wind words, the Spirit blowing through the churches" (Revelation 2:7 MSG). The wind words are not carved in stone like the law which God gave Moses. Instead, wind words are like the gentle whisper with which God spoke to Elijah "After the earthquake a fire, but the Lord was not in the fire; and after the fire a sound of a gentle blowing" (1 Kings 19:11–13). The Spirit speaks wind words as a gentle blowing.

The intensity of a sound relates to the amount of energy it contains. A sound with more energy has higher intensity and is considered to be louder, like thunder. The Spirit's high-energy words are creative and revealing. His words filled with the highest levels of energy produce creative miracles. God spoke the universe into existence (Hebrews 11:3). His words created everything seen. Every creature is an expression of God's word.

The Spirit's words which reveal a person's calling are full of energy. This energy may be manifested in special ways, making a person's calling particularly memorable. As Saul traveled to

HEARING THE SPIRIT'S VOICE

Damascus, a bright light flashed around him and he was called to be a servant and a witness for Jesus (Acts 26:12–18). The words spoken by the Spirit in revealing a calling may bring light and life to a specific scripture or instruction. As prophets are touched by the Spirit in hearing their calling, they may be moved in their hearts to activate this calling. Powerful feelings within will compel them to do what God wants done. This is passion.

The sound of the Spirit's voice is on a supernatural frequency, which is outside the range heard by natural ears. Frequency relates to the number of sound waves or energy surges per second. The sound of distant thunder has a low frequency, while a whistle has a high frequency. The pitch of a voice rises and falls with frequency. People have high pitched voices when they are anxious, weary or trying to persuade others. The flesh, the world and the devil often use persuasive voices with high pitches, trying to get people to follow them. The Lord is at rest with everything under control, so the Spirit's voice is generally soft, gentle and low. The Lord, my shepherd, "makes me lie down in green pastures; he leads me beside quiet waters" (Psalm 23:1–2). When spiritual people heard words from heaven, the natural people around them could not understand what was said (John 12:28–29).

The Spirit has a unique voice, like every person has a unique voice. But different people may hear him differently. The Spirit speaks in different tones for different purposes. He speaks with low, authoritative tones to bring correction and soft, gentle tones to bring comfort. Softer tones appear more friendly and helpful. The Spirit may use soft tones to guide a person. Low tones are associated with authority and truth. The Spirit often speaks with low, authoritative tones to bring correction. When he speaks with these tones, there is no question about his meaning. Correction is not enjoyable at the time, but when heeded it brings peace (Hebrews 12:11).

Conductor of the Spirit's Words

The conductor through which the Spirit's words travel is not air or any other natural thing. There is no continuous, natural conductor between heaven where God is enthroned and earth where people want to hear from him. The Spirit's words travel through a spiritual conductor known in the word of God as "in the spirit". The word spirit is not capitalized in this phrase, because it relates to the spiritual realm rather than God's Spirit. "God is spirit, and those who worship him must worship in spirit and truth" (John 4:24). The term in the spirit means "a state of deep spiritual communion with God" (Revelation 1:10 EXB). Religious people called Christ the son of David, but in the spirit David exalted him as Lord (Matthew 22:42–44). John was in the spirit when he heard a voice instruct him to write down a vision and then send it to the churches (Revelation 1:10–11). As prophets walk in the spirit, they stay in a position to hear the Spirit's words.

Receivers of the Spirit's Words

A natural man can hear natural sounds but not spiritual sounds. The natural man does not perceive the things of the Spirit (1 Corinthians 2:14). Jesus knew many would not hear spiritual truths. He repeatedly made the statement, "If anyone has ears to hear, let him hear" (Mark 4:23 and 7:16). Although the people around him had natural ears, few had spiritual ears tuned to the correct frequency. He was talking about people who could listen to the frequency on which God was speaking by his Spirit.

HEARING THE SPIRIT'S VOICE

As Isaiah the prophet wrote, two things open people's ears to spiritual truths: salvation and discipleship. First, when people are saved or converted through the new birth, their heart is changed, and they can understand spiritual truth. Behold, the Lord come to save and "the eyes of the blind will be opened and the ears of the deaf will be unstopped (Isaiah 35:4–5). This scripture refers both to physical and spiritual ears. When people are saved, they may be able to recognize the voice of the Spirit speaking. However, they may not hear his voice very often until they are prepared to hear it.

Second, when people become disciplined learners, they can understand spiritual truths. A disciple of Jesus embraces his word. The Lord "awakens my ear to listen as a disciple" (Isaiah 50:4–5). As believers diligently seek spiritual things, their ears become tuned to the Spirit's wind words. When they put the kingdom first by studying the word of God and seeking spiritual things, they became more sensitive to the voice of the Spirit.

A prophet's heart has to be prepared to consistently hear the Spirit's words. These words are received by the spirit of the prophet and transmitted to the mind. Spiritual ears hear his words, not natural ears. It takes spiritual ears tuned to the Spirit's frequency in order to consistently hear wind words.

While the Spirit can speak to babes in Christ, his words are heard best by trained spiritual ears and understood best by renewed minds. Spiritual ears and a renewed mind are products of spiritual growth, which relinquishes the flesh. Hearing the Spirit is directly related to the spiritual growth of the prophet. A prophet's spiritual ears must be trained to hear what the Spirit is saying. This can be done by knowing the word of God and experiencing his presence.

Personal Story about Training Spiritual Ears

I am one of Jesus' sheep and I hear his voice. I trained my spiritual ears to hear the Spirit by relying on Jesus' promise I could hear his voice. Jesus said, "My sheep hear my voice" (John 10:27). Many times, I told Jesus, "I am one of your sheep, and I hear your voice." I became more and more sensitive to the Spirit over time. I began to act on the scripture about being one of his sheep. My pastors came to our town to visit and pray with people in the hospital. I asked the Lord to let me know when they were coming so I could meet them at the hospital. One evening after dinner as I was cleaning the kitchen, I heard the Spirit say my pastors were on their way to the hospital. Quickly, I told my husband I had to go to the hospital. I drove into the parking lot right behind my pastors and began to walk with them. My pastor smiled and told me I was learning. It was so exciting to know I heard from the Spirit.

Conclusions

The Spirit speaks often to his prophets. Their knowing how to hear his voice is important for them to speak for him. His words are supernatural and filled with boundless energy. He speaks on a frequency which cannot be heard normally by the natural ear. When he speaks to a prophet, his words are heard by the spirit of the prophet. Tuning the spiritual ears to his frequency requires spiritual growth. Staying tuned to his frequency involves a lifestyle committed to the Lord. He uses different tones of voice to correct, comfort and guide. Stay tuned to his frequency and listen closely for the tone of his voice. Speak the Spirit's message using the proper tone to convey the fullness of the message.

CHAPTER 6
NATURE OF THE PROPHET

My prophets walk in love, speak the truth in love and demonstrate my unconditional love to my children. Their faith is activated by my love, and by my love they are protected from all enemies. They are trees of righteousness which bring forth their fruit in due season. Their motivation is not their own selves but is for my will to be accomplished.

Prophets are known by their fruit, not their gifts. They are filled to overflowing with love, joy, peace and all other fruit of the Spirit. Without love, the prophetic gift cannot operate (1 Corinthians 13:2 AMP). The prophetic voice is an expression of the greatest love which Jesus demonstrated by his death on the cross. "Greater love has no one than this, that one lay down his life for his friends" (John 15:13). Prophets demonstrate this same great love. "This is my commandment, that you love one another, just as I have loved you" (John 15:12). This chapter examines the greatest love, showing how love is developed and expressed through the prophetic voice. A true prophet is motivated by love and prophesies in proportion to his/her faith (Romans 12:6).

The Greatest Love: Spirit of Excellence

Desire love above the prophetic gift. Love is God's excellent way of life. "Earnestly desire the greater gifts, and I show you a still more excellent way" (1 Corinthians 12:31). The spirit of excellence is the spirit of love, the spirit of power and the mind of Christ. God has given us a spirit "of power and of love and of a sound mind" (2 Timothy 1:7 NKJV). The sound mind to which this verse refers is the mind of Christ, because believers have been given the mind of Christ (1 Corinthians 2:16). The Spirit brings forth the spirit of love, the spirit of power and the mind of Christ in a prophet to form the spirit of excellence. The spirit of the prophet is to be conformed to the image of Christ as expressed by this spirit of excellence.

The Spirit works through prophets, bringing authority and abundance to the spirit of the prophet. The spirit of the prophet is filled with heaven's wisdom and might. It is a vessel of anointing and power to proclaim the gospel of the kingdom and to set the captives free. The spirit of the prophet is favored by God and man. The Lord's favor on people causes others to favor them, as well. The favor of the Lord and man is upon those people who live by the truth and show mercy and kindness (Proverbs 3:3–4).

Prophets operate in the supernatural love realm, which the scriptures refer to as the fourth dimension. To help understand this concept, consider the dimensions of things in this world. A map on a piece of paper has only two dimensions. A building has three dimensions, and this world has three dimensions. The greatest love, which is not of this world, has four dimensions. It is possible to know the breadth, length, height and depth of the love of Christ (Ephesians 3:17–19). One-dimensional love relates to loving oneself. Two-dimensional love relates to loving your own family.

Three-dimensional love relates to loving your own church and those of your culture. Four-dimensional love relates to loving the lost and dying world. The love of Christ is described as having four dimensions, which makes it unlike the things of this world. Natural love cannot approach the fourth dimension of the love of Christ. It cannot be compared with the love of Christ. The natural mind cannot comprehend the love of Christ.

Fred and I had a mission downtown for eight years. It was in the mission where we experienced this fourth dimension of love. The homeless, drunkards, prostitutes and drug addicts came through the mission needing many things. The Spirit poured the love of Christ into our hearts, and we began to love the way Jesus loves. We love people who do not act like us, smell like us, talk like us or look like us. A person's mind can be renewed to the word of God to see into the love of Christ. The Spirit searches the deep things of God and shows them to us (1 Corinthians 2: 10).

Daniel's Spirit of Excellence

Much can be learned about the spirit of the prophet by studying the life of the prophet Daniel, who had an excellent spirit (Daniel 6:3). His highest priority was serving the Lord. Daniel was chosen from the captured Israelite nobility and prepared to serve the king of Babylon (Daniel 1–2). He was chosen for his wisdom, knowledge and understanding. Daniel purposed in his heart to serve the Lord. The Lord gave Daniel an unusual aptitude for learning and the ability to understand visions and dreams. The favor of the Lord, as well as, kings was upon Daniel. He was promoted to positions of great authority and was influential in the royal courts of both Babylon and Persia.

Daniel understood the importance of the prophetic voice. By studying the word of God, he knew when it was time for the fulfillment of Jeremiah's prophecy for the return of the people of Israel to their homeland (Jeremiah 25:11; Daniel 9:1–19). He prayed for this prophecy to be fulfilled, and God answered his prayer.

Prophets who operate with a spirit of excellence have an unusual ability for learning and understanding visions and dreams. They understand the operation and importance of the prophetic voice, and the favor of the Lord is upon them. When these prophets hear from the Lord and know what he wants to do, they declare it and proclaim it into the earth.

Developing Love as a Spirit of Excellence

The Holy Spirit deposits the greatest love in the spirit of the prophet. Three conditions are needed for a prophet to truly love and develop a spirit of excellence: pure heart, good conscience and sincere faith. "The goal of our instruction is love from a pure heart and a good conscience and a sincere faith" (1 Timothy 1:5). Purity is needed for the prophet to hear and see the Father. "Blessed are the pure in heart, for they shall see God" (Matthew 5:8). A prophet's conscience is the voice of the spirit of the prophet, bearing witness with what is right and what is wrong. If a prophet is not condemned by his/her conscience, he/she has confidence in hearing God's voice. "If our heart does not condemn us, we have confidence before God" (1 John 3:21). Renewing the mind to the anointed word of God produces the mind of Christ in a prophet. "Put on the new self, which in the likeness of God has been created in righteousness and holiness of the truth" (Ephesians 4:24).

Demonstrating Love as a Spirit of Excellence

The spirit of the prophet manifests the fruit of the Spirit, including love, joy and peace (Galatians 5:22–23). The prophet ministers to King Jesus before ministering to others. The prophetic gifts of the Spirit operate through the spirit of excellence. Excellence is not defeating your enemy; excellence loves your enemy. Excellence is not cursing; excellence is blessing those who curse you.

Prayer

The prophet is a prayer warrior who prays for the Father's will to be accomplished in the earth. Daniel fasted and prayed, seeking the Lord's will and help. Daniel openly prayed and gave thanks and continually served the Lord (Daniel 6:10, 16). The Lord sent his angel to open Daniel's understanding, so he would know God was answering his prayer. Prayer is critical for understanding the Father's will and bringing it forth on the earth. It is the backbone of everything God is doing.

Forgiveness

Prophets have been persecuted throughout the ages, and they will continue to be persecuted. "Which one of the prophets did your fathers not persecute?" (Acts 7:52) If prophets internalize persecution, the hurts will burden their lives and hinder their ministries. Failure to forgive anyone creates bondage which is accompanied by all manner of negative emotions. Nothing good comes from any bondage. Prophets need to know how to respond to persecution. Those who rejoice over being persecuted for righteousness sake will receive the same great reward as all the prophets who were persecuted before them (Matthew 5:10–12). A critical response to persecution is forgiveness.

Forgiveness is patterned after the Father's forgiveness. It takes the Spirit to enable believers to forgive just as the Father forgives.

Forgiveness releases both parties from bondage. When believers let the Spirit help them forgive, their spirits are set free.

Jesus taught forgiveness (Matthew 6:14). He declared forgiveness over the paralyzed man's sins before he healed him (Mark 2:5–11). Forgiveness comes first by faith and then people can be made whole. The blood of Jesus makes the conscience pure, taking away even the memory of hurts (Hebrews 9:14). There is no limit on forgiveness. Peter thought seven times would be the maximum number of times to forgive someone. However, Jesus said to forgive seventy times seven (Matthew 18:21–22). Be quick to forgive those who persecute you or hurt you in any way.

Sometimes, we instruct people to write down who they want to forgive and then throw away the paper. A simple deed like this can help activate faith for forgiveness. Even if it takes time for negative emotions to leave, they can remember the paper and the time they activated faith rather than remembering the hurt.

In a church service where I was ministering several years ago, the Lord moved mightily and healed many. In particular, a woman who was scheduled for heart surgery the next day was slain in the spirit and healed. When she got up off the floor, she said God had healed her heart. As I was leaving the service, a woman came running up to me with her fist doubled up. She was about to hit me in the face. She said I was a false prophet because I wore makeup and jewelry. Two men stopped her from hitting me and safely escorted me to my car. By the way, the woman with the heart condition never had heart surgery and is still healed today. On the way home, I forgave the angry woman and asked God to forgive her.

True Giving

Joyous giving without requiring anything in return is a demonstration of Christ's love. His sacrificial giving is the pattern for true giving. Although Jesus Christ was rich, he became poor so that you might become rich (2 Corinthians 8:9). God's prophets follow his example of giving by committing everything to the Lord. They realize everything they possess has been given to them by the Lord (1 Corinthians 4:7). He has placed some of his possessions in their hands as a steward over them. Realizing they are only stewards over his possessions, they can be led by the Holy Spirit in their giving and give from a pure heart. The Lord is more concerned with how they give (the condition of their heart and their motives) than he is with what they give. Jesus said the widow who offered two small copper coins gave more than those who gave large offerings for the wrong reasons (Mark 12:41–44). He knew things in their hearts were not right. The Lord is looking for purity and purpose in the hearts of his prophets. True riches are more than material things. The true riches include such eternal things as salvation, word of life, fruit of the Spirit and gifts of the Spirit. Giving the true riches out of purpose and purity is true giving.

Giving gives me great joy. I remember the times we took food down on the street for the runaways, homeless and prostitutes. As I gave out the food, I always asked if they needed prayer. Many of the people wanted prayer and an encouraging word from the Lord. I gave them what I had from the Holy Spirit. They were given physical food and spiritual food. They went away happy and knowing someone cared what they were going through.

Personal Story about God's Love

God's love can be demonstrated in many ways. Our ministry started with loving the children. Every week we went to low-income areas and presented the gospel of Jesus to the children. The children climbed up in our laps and wanted us to sing to them. This is love. They went home and told their parents. Before long their parents came to hear about Jesus. God told me people could not resist his love. We found this to be true. God's love is powerful.

Conclusions

Jesus manifested the greatest love through his death on the cross. The most excellent way of life demonstrates this same great love. When the Spirit deposits the greatest love in the heart of a prophet, the spirit of the prophet becomes a spirit of excellence. Everything done by a prophet with the spirit of excellence is motivated by love. The prophet is known by love, not by the gift. Even when the gift does not operate, love endures and never fails. The spirit of excellence desires to do the Father's will and live the life of Christ by his faith with great power and authority. Excellence loves! Excellence overcomes by love, not by fighting.

CHAPTER 7
EMPOWERING THE PROPHETIC VOICE

My energy and power flow throughout the heavens and the earth. There are those in my church who I have empowered to establish my kingdom on the earth. They have the power to enter into my presence and receive from me a supernatural strength. They go throughout the earth sowing and reaping by my power, says the Lord.

God's prophets are empowered with supernatural authority and power to effectively work in the kingdom. When empowered, they become a transformer of God's power, releasing supernatural power into the natural realm. Prophets are empowered as they mature. This chapter examines God's provision for maturing and empowering prophets.

Empowered by the Spirit

Supernatural power equips prophets to do the work of the kingdom. This power, which is from heaven, comes through the Spirit. The disciples were not permitted to advance the kingdom until they were given power from heaven (Luke 24:49). "You will receive power when the Holy Spirit has come upon you" (Acts 1:8).

The Spirit is a storehouse of great power. As he abides in prophets, they have this power in their spirits. He empowers prophets to move into the supernatural realm and do exploits. This power is released by faith to do the work of the kingdom. "If your gift is prophesying, then prophesy in accordance with your faith (Romans 12:6 NIV). Speaking the word of God and praying can cause an explosion of power.

Developing a strong relationship with the Spirit helps prophets hear and recognize his voice. Becoming sensitive to his voice is a sign of maturity. "For all who are being led by the Spirit of God, these are sons of God" (Romans 8:14). Mature prophets consistently follow the guidance of the Spirit. They hear, see and know by the Spirit.

As prophets yield to the Spirit, they have more power available to do the work of the kingdom. Those who are filled with God's power can overcome adversities. His power will fully equip prophets for all situations.

Empowered by the Word of God

Jesus has all authority in heaven and earth (Matthew 28:18). He delegates his authority to those whom he calls to work in his kingdom. The only kingdom authority prophets have is delegated authority. This authority is revealed to them through the word of God, which is Jesus. "In the beginning was the word, and the word was with God, and the word was God" (John 1:1). The word of God is powerful, and it empowers those who believe. "The word that God speaks is alive and full of power" (Hebrews 4:12 AMP). The amount of authority prophets actually walk in depends on their understanding and applying the word.

The word of God is precious like gold. As prophets seek the truth in the word and act on the word, it becomes powerful to them. It will defeat every enemy and bring life, peace and prosperity. All things were created by speaking the word of God in faith. Prophets need this power as they move in the supernatural realm. The devil is against the prophetic voice being released into the earth, because he knows the word carries the power to accomplish God's will.

Spiritual growth involves the process of enlightenment, revelation and application. Some people are being enlightened and given revelation of the word of God but never taught to apply it. Faith becomes effective only by acting on the word. Understanding and applying the word help empower prophets to do the work of the kingdom.

Empowered by Spiritual Relationships

Prophets are empowered with authority by being under authority to spiritual leaders. The centurion, who recognized authority comes from being under authority, was characterized as having great faith (Matthew 8:5–13). Christ gave the five-fold ministry gifts to mature prophets so they can live in harmony together. Those spiritual leaders help nurture and train prophets. They exhibit a spirit of humility as they guide prophets and even restore those who have done something wrong.

There is a spiritual order in the body of Christ. "God has placed in the church first of all apostles, second prophets, third teachers, then miracles, then gifts of healing, of helping, of guidance, and of different kinds of tongues" (1 Corinthians 12:28 NIV). Lower-order gifts such as teachers and pastors are neither ordained nor equipped to mature higher-order gifts such as apostles and prophets. Apostles and prophets develop and release other prophets. Young prophets are often frustrated with their relationships with pastors who are not ordained of God to develop and release prophets. Prophets need relationships with apostles and other prophets.

An apostle or prophet who takes on a nurturing role for a prophet over a long period of time becomes a spiritual father to him/her. Spiritual fathers have the heavenly Father's heart to bring forth sons. Joseph was a spiritual father to Pharaoh. He said, "God has made me a father to Pharaoh and lord of all his household and ruler over all the land of Egypt" (Genesis 45:8). Elijah was a spiritual father to Elisha. When Elijah was taken up in the fiery chariots, Elisha cried out "My father, my father, the chariots of Israel and its horsemen!" (2 Kings 2:12). In the New Testament, Joseph was a spiritual father to Jesus, and Paul was a spiritual father to Timothy, Titus and others. As a spiritual father, Paul labored in prayer for those he called his children so they would mature. He desired Christ to be manifested in their lives (Galatians 4:19).

Paul wrote there are few spiritual fathers but many tutors (1 Corinthians 4:14–15). A tutor supervises the life and morals of children but does not have the heart of a father to mature them. A tutor serves only to direct and instruct the children, showing them the true way. Spiritual fathers are needed to bring believers into their purpose and destiny. Maturity comes from the anointing and gifts of the spiritual fathers. In the last days, the hearts of the fathers will be turned to the sons and the hearts of the sons will be turned to the fathers (Malachi 4:6).

Prophets are encouraged to mature in the Lord and be empowered to walk in authority and fulfill destiny. A spiritual father helps prophets mature and can impart things into their lives which could not be obtained from anyone else. God has a spiritual father for every prophet. Failure to identify and join God's ordained spiritual father will hinder a prophet's spiritual growth.

Spiritual fathers help protect prophets from destruction. Many prophets have been destroyed, because they were isolated from the body of Christ and did not recognize the importance of godly relationships. The Spirit will show prophets those relationships ordained of the Lord to propel them into their destiny.

Personal Story about God's Power

There are times in my life when the power of God moves down through my arms and hands. This gives me the assurance me the Spirit has empowered me to act on his word. In Spain I was told by the Lord to do something I had never done before. His instructions related to a young woman with a heart problem who could hardly walk. As she was being brought to the platform, the Spirit said, "Lie on top of her, and I will breathe life into her heart". Just like Elijah lay on top of the boy (1 Kings 17:21), I lay on the young woman, and immediately I felt the power of God go through my whole body. I knew God's energy went out of me and into her. God healed her heart. She jumped up and began to leap and cry out she was strong and healed.

Conclusions

There is great power within a prophet's spirit. It is the Holy Spirit. He empowers prophets to do exploits and operate in the supernatural realm. This power within the spirit of the prophet must be released by faith to do the work of the kingdom.

Through the Spirit, prophets can reach out and touch the supernatural realm. Their dreams and purpose can be a reality when they are empowered with God's strength and hope. The presence of God within prophets gives them strength and power. They will be empowered to defeat every enemy when they worship the Lord in spirit and in truth.

The more of the Spirit which is within prophets, the more power they have to do the work of the kingdom. Prophets who are filled with power can overcome every obstacle. God's power equips prophets for all situations. God empowers prophets to empower others.

CHAPTER 8
SPIRITUAL GIFTS OF THE PROPHET

Desire spiritual gifts for they will bring comfort, peace and hope. The gifts are different, but all are given by the Holy Spirit. My gifts come from the spiritual realm and are true, says the Lord. They only operate by love and are my love poured out from my heart.

The gift of prophecy is common to all prophets, but they also operate other spiritual gifts. They consistently operate three gifts: prophecy, discerning of spirits and word of knowledge. They are encouraged to operate in more gifts (1 Corinthians 12:31). Spiritual gifts can complement prophecy and increase the impact of prophets. God's plan for spiritual gifts is aimed at the greater good and involves their widespread use in everyday life. They can be used in the home, the marketplace and the workplace, as well as on the streets. This chapter examines the operation of spiritual gifts.

Even as a child, I knew things about what had happened to people and what was about to happen. I did not ask to know these things, but I knew them by the Spirit. At such an early age I did not know what to do with this information. Operation of spiritual gifts has intensified in my life in recent times. The Spirit told me he would increase my abilities as a warring prophetess to combat and expel the evil and darkness, because gross darkness is coming fast upon the earth. When the Spirit shows me things, I quickly respond with prayer and action. Also, in recent times my eyes have become more sensitive to the spiritual realm. At times I can see inside of a person's body and know exactly what needs to be corrected. The Lord has healed the sick and performed miracles as I speak out what I see.

Introducing Spiritual Gifts

The gifts of the Spirit hear and see what God is doing in the spirit and what he wants to do in the natural realm. Spiritual gifts can be grouped into three broad categories.

- Hear and see the spiritual realm.
- Speak what was heard.
- Do what was seen.

Jesus spoke only what he heard the Father say, and he did only what he saw the Father do (John 5:19; 8:26).

The inspirational gifts are word of knowledge, word of wisdom and discerning of spirits (1 Corinthians 12:8 and 10). The word of knowledge makes a fact known which was not known in the natural. For example, a word of knowledge may point out a person with a particular ailment. The Spirit makes this fact known to correct the ailment. The word of wisdom gives supernatural direction to a person or group. In general, wisdom gives understanding on how to use knowledge. Discerning of spirits can see angelic beings and/or evil spirits.

On a consistent basis, the gift of discerning of spirits is in operation in my life. I have seen both angels and demonic forces. Some of the angels have been those who are sent to carry people from this world to the next. They are all tall and without wings. They stand ready in hospital rooms or bedrooms. I have also seen warring angels, those with swords ready to war against the forces of evil. The demonic forces I have seen have been snakes, lizards and other creatures. They have been primarily green. Some have had huge teeth. The Spirit of the Lord always shows me what to do and what to say to these forces.

The verbal gifts are tongues, interpretation of tongues and prophecy (1 Corinthians 12:10). These gifts build up the body of Christ. The gift of tongues is a public utterance of a heavenly language when people are assembled together, and it has to be interpreted for the people to understand. The gift of interpretation of tongues provides understanding to what was said in the heavenly language. In contrast to the gift of tongues, the believer's prayer language is generally considered as a private prayer language used to build up his/her own faith. "But you, beloved, building yourselves up on your most holy faith, praying in the Holy Spirit" (Jude 1:20). Any believer who is filled with the Holy Spirit can pray in the spirit without having to interpret the message. The gift of prophecy is equivalent to the use of both tongues and the interpretation of tongues, because prophecy can be understood by the people. It builds up faith in the people.

The power gifts are faith, healing and miracles (1 Corinthians 12:9–10). The measure of faith which is given to every believer might be considered as the common faith in contrast to the spiritual gift of faith. "God has allotted to each a measure of faith" (Romans 12:3). The gift of faith is a powerful force which magnifies a believer's common faith. The gift of faith is used for others when their faith is weak or they cannot activate their own faith. The gift of miracles is the unlimited miraculous power which can change natural situations. Miracles happen when God supernaturally intervenes. While believers can have faith to be healed and faith to pray for others to be healed, the gifts of healing release tremendous healing power beyond what an individual already believes.

The gifts of the Spirit flow out of the love of God. They show forth his glory and his majesty. Spiritual gifts operate in love and by faith (1 Corinthians 13:1–2; Hebrews 11:6). All the gifts operate by the Spirit (1 Corinthians 12:11). God wants his spiritual gifts to operate through believers, but they are particularly prominent among prophets. Opportunities to help others with these gifts may exist in any place. Wherever prophets are loving people, they can operate in the gifts. God is looking for a willing vessel, someone who yields to his will.

Those people who are interested in building up the body of Christ will accept spiritual gifts and consent to the Spirit's moving through them. People who resist the Spirit and spiritual gifts serve their rigid doctrines above the truth. Such negative attitudes hinder the work of God. Spiritual gifts are for everyone, but the people have to trust God before they can receive the gifts.

Purpose of Spiritual Gifts

Spiritual gifts are given to be used for God's glory. Speak the utterances of God and serve others "so that in all things God may be glorified through Jesus Christ" (1 Peter 4:11). They are to be used to help each other. "As each one has received a special gift, employ it in serving one another as good stewards of the manifold grace of God" (1 Peter 4:10). Spiritual gifts are given to each person for the common good or benefit of all people (1 Corinthians 12:7).

Spiritual gifts bring the lost into the kingdom of God. They look upon the signs and wonders and declare there is a God and they want to be with him (1 Corinthians 14:24–25). Jesus compels believers to go into the highways and byways telling people to come into the kingdom of God, not into a particular congregation or denomination. Those people who are willing to let the spiritual gifts flow through them can be very effective in reaching the lost.

Spiritual gifts help the saints and build up the body of Christ. Anyone who shares a spiritual gift in a meeting should build up the church (1 Corinthians 14:26). "For you can all prophesy one by one, so that all may learn and all may be exhorted" (1 Corinthians 14:31).

Receiving Spiritual Gifts

A gift can be offered to someone, but it becomes a blessing only when it is received. Spiritual gifts can be received by a person acting on the word of God alone or allowing others to pray for him/her to receive the gifts. Paul described how spiritual leaders prayed for Timothy and imparted a spiritual gift to him. They prophesied over him and laid hands on him so he could receive the gift. "Do not neglect the spiritual gift within you, which was bestowed on you through prophetic utterance with the laying on of hands by the presbytery" (1 Timothy 4:14). Prophets have to be willing vessels for spiritual gifts to operate through them. Without faith it is impossible to please God (Hebrews 11:6). Natural thoughts about personal inabilities and limitations will hinder the flow of spiritual gifts through a prophet. The vessels through which God chooses to deliver his gifts are frail, but the source of these gifts is holy and perfect. Recognizing every good and perfect gift is from above will help prophets operate in spiritual gifts.

Activating Spiritual Gifts

Prophets can expect spiritual gifts to operate through them. When the gifts are being activated at first, they can ask for instructions and help from spiritual leaders, pray for divine guidance for themselves and put a demand on the spiritual gifts within them. Spiritual leaders have insight on the gifts within the people and how to activate the gifts. "For this reason I remind you to kindle afresh the gift of God which is in you through the laying on of my hands" (2 Timothy 1:6). It is important to have supportive leaders around people as they are learning to operate spiritual gifts to show them when and how to operate the gifts.

We help young people develop and activate spiritual gifts by providing a safe environment in which they can prophesy and pray for people. Small group settings work well for these spiritual efforts. We instruct them about prophecy, give them opportunities to prophesy to one another and give them gentle feedback on their efforts to operate in the supernatural realm. Their initial efforts may seem small, but such efforts can help them gain confidence they are hearing from the Spirit and prophesying those things which are worthwhile to others.

Personal Story about Prophesying to the Lost

One summer day when I was feeding the homeless on the street, a teenage boy came up for a hot dog but got much more. The Spirit of God rose up inside me, activating the word of knowledge. The Lord began to tell this boy how he was beaten with a leather strap by his dad until he ran away from home. Then the Spirit shared the story of Jesus and how he was beaten and how he loved this teenager. This teenager began to cry and accepted Jesus as savior right there on the street.

Conclusions

Everyone can offer himself/herself to be used as a vessel through which spiritual gifts flow. A person can seek the Lord to identify his/her own calling and gifts. Spiritual relationships can help identify and confirm a person's calling and gifts. Spiritual gifts are received by faith and operated by faith.

Opportunities to be used of the Lord exist everywhere. As people make themselves aware of the spiritual realm and what the Lord wants to do through them, they will be used mightily by the Lord in his kingdom. Those who earnestly pursue spiritual gifts will be a blessing to others and fulfill their own calling.

CHAPTER 9
PROPHETIC IMPACTS

This is the time, says the Lord, for my prophets to reveal my plan. They will proclaim it from the rooftops. They will expose the evil and corruption and bring forth the truth. The truth will set my people free.

God will not move without a powerful prophetic voice in the earth, and the body of Christ cannot build properly without it. The prophetic voice has far-reaching impacts throughout the kingdom of God. This chapter examines the impacts of the prophetic voice. The prophetic impacts identified here would be missing in the body of Christ if the prophetic voice is rejected or silent.

Reveals God's Plans

The prophetic voice is an expression of God's will on the earth. The Spirit shows the mysteries of God to the prophets, as well as the apostles (Ephesians 3:4–5). They hear the Spirit, flow with the Spirit and show the deep things of God to his people. They are messengers of God who are responsible for speaking his will into the earth.

Prophets have an uncommon commitment to the greater good. They have a revelation of the body of Christ and see the body as a whole rather than just part of it. They have a revelation of the kingdom of God which is broader than the body of Christ. The Spirit is giving a fresh revelation to his prophets.

They reach forth their hands and lay them upon others so they may know God truly. He has called the prophets to go forth into the dark places to bring out his apostles, prophets, evangelists, pastors and teachers who are in hiding. One day when we were ministering in a prison about the prophetic voice, we asked which of the men had a prophetic calling on their lives. Sixteen men on the first row acknowledged their prophetic calling. Without knowing who had a prophetic calling, these sixteen men sought seats on the first row, because they wanted to be near the anointing. They had been running from God, but it was time for them to answer their calling.

As the Lord spoke to his prophets of old, he is speaking to his prophets today. He will hide nothing from the prophets. He will reveal himself but not in a cloud, lightning or a burning bush. He will speak to his prophets face to face. The time has come to show Jesus to the people, and the prophets have a critical role in revealing the truth about Jesus.

Builds Foundation

The kingdom of God is built on a strong foundation. Along with the apostles, the prophets build the foundation on Jesus Christ, the Chief Cornerstone (Ephesians 2:20). The prophets lay out the pattern for the building. They show believers the kingdom of God exists within them now rather than it being just a new kingdom which will come sometime in the future. The prophetic voice helps believers operate in the kingdom.

The prophetic voice brings life, hope, comfort and increase. Bringing comfort and hope help establish the hearts of people. The prophetic voice can heal the brokenhearted.

The prophetic voice helps believers hear the Spirit speak to them by confirming whether they truly are hearing the Spirit. Believers have to recognize when the Spirit is speaking to them before they can move forward in purpose and destiny. God's prophets work with other five-fold ministry gifts to bring spirituality and maturity to the saints (Ephesians 4:11–12). Experiencing the true prophetic gift helps believers understand the spiritual realm and distinguish between spiritual and carnal things.

We kept trying to fit into other congregations and ministries until we heard the prophetic voice. In each congregation, we first would start working with young children, later with the youth and finally with adults, hoping someone would recognize our gifts and callings and release us. These traditional congregations only wanted us to help them fulfill their purpose with no consideration for ours. When we found the kingdom joints God ordained for us, the apostles and prophets laid hands on us, prophesied over us and released us into our ministry. They released us into our purpose and destiny and helped us walk in them.

Gives Direction

The prophetic voice gives divine direction to individuals, groups and/or the body of Christ as a whole. The apostle first brings authority and then the prophet comes in with direction. The prophet cannot override the apostle, because these two ministry gifts work together. Both gifts have been missing in the body of

Christ. Consequently, the body has had neither God's authority nor his direction.

Prophets help define vision and purpose. They give personal prophecy to individuals and prophetic words for the whole body of Christ. They are able to confirm what the Spirit of God is saying to the people.

Some prophetic words include a call to action. For example, the prophet Elisha sent word to the leper Naaman with instructions on what he needed to do to be healed. "Go and wash in the Jordan seven times, and your flesh will be restored to you and you will be clean" (2 Kings 5:10). If he washed in any other river, he would not be healed. Only by following the prophetic call to action was Naaman healed. The prophetic call to action is the definitive answer to any problem. With a command people have no choice; the commands of a king are to be obeyed. People are held accountable for not obeying such commands. With a prophetic call to action people have a choice: they can follow the call or fail to follow it. Failure to follow a call to action does not bring judgment, but following a call to action brings positive benefits like healing.

Drives Back Evil

Prophets confront evil with the word of God, calling sin what it really is rather than letting it remain unchecked. When the prophetic voice exposes sin, the people are led to repentance and redemption. As people are brought to the point of repentance, they are given an opportunity to change their ways. God gives the gift of repentance which brings refreshing and revival (Acts 3:19). When people repent, they leave the place of lusting for their own selfishness and move to the place where they desire the things of the

Lord. Many times in jail and prison services, we lead the prisoners in repentance so they can freely receive everything the Lord has for them.

God sends his prophets to call churches, cities and nations to repentance from evil and carnality. Jonah's prophetic message brought repentance to the city of Nineveh (Jonah 3:1–9). "When God saw their deeds, that they turned from their wicked way, then God relented concerning the calamity which he had declared he would bring upon them" (Jonah 3:10). Revivals in cities and nations depend on their hearing the true prophetic voice.

The prophetic voice stops the enemy. Jesus stood up in a sinking boat and rebuked the storm (Matthew 8:23–27). God in his mercy is sending his prophets to combat religious spirits like the spirit of python, which squeezes out the spiritual life. Jesus cast a legion of demons out of a madman (Mark 5:2–15). The prophets have authority over all demons. Prophets are engaged in spiritual warfare, teaching and leading others to defeat their enemies so they can walk in victory, healing and prosperity.

I remember going into three crack houses and rescuing those held captive by drugs, one being my very own son. Inside the houses, needles were on the floor, people were crashed on the floor and clothing was everywhere. The darkness, evil and smell took my breath away, but the Lord said he was with me so I did what he told me to do. Evil could not hold these people when Jesus showed up on the scene. God's goodness overcomes every evil.

Releases Potential

The prophetic sees the invisible and brings those things into their time dimension. Just like the prophet Abraham saw Jesus' day and rejoiced in it, prophets bring forth the new (John 8:56). The prophetic calls those things which are not as though they were.

The prophetic voice creates opportunities which otherwise would not exist. For example, when the prophetic voice uttered, the gate of the besieged city opened wide (2 Kings 6 and 7). Samaria was under siege and the people needed relief from famine and destruction. The prophet Elisha gave a prophetic word about food prices being much lower on the following day (2 Kings 7:1). When Elisha released the prophetic word, a shift occurred. The following day the enemy army which had surrounded the city fled before the Lord, and food prices fell dramatically.

Prophets impart spiritual gifts, along with others ministers. The word of God explains how Timothy had received a spiritual gift as elders laid hands on him and gave prophetic utterances (1 Timothy 4:14).. Paul wrote to believers in Rome, "I long to see you so that I may impart some spiritual gift to you, that you may be established" (Romans 1:11). It is important for believers to find those spiritual relationships ordained of God so they can receive the spiritual gifts God intends for them.

Obedience to a prophetic word can bring victory in any situation. For example, when an army invaded Judah the people asked for the Lord's help and a prophet spoke a prophetic word which brought them victory (2 Chronicles 20). The prophetic word gave instructions to Judah on where to go against the enemy and what to do. Judah first sent out singers to praise the Lord, and then the Lord ambushed their enemies and gave them the victory.

Those who put their trust in the Lord's prophets will succeed (2 Chronicles 20:20).

Personal Stories on Victory over Evil

I remember going into three crack houses and rescuing those held captive by drugs, one being my very own son. Inside the houses, needles were on the floor, people were crashed on the floor and clothing was everywhere. The darkness, evil and smell took my breath away, but the Lord told me he was with me so I did what he told me to do. Evil could not hold these people when Jesus showed up on the scene. God's goodness overcomes every evil.

One day I was called to the bedside of a woman who was dying. She had stopped eating and would not respond to any one. As I was praying for her, I felt a presence behind me breathing over me. I thought her husband had come back into the room. When I turned around, I saw an evil spirit which said he had been sent to kill the woman. In the name of Jesus I commanded the evil spirit to leave and broke his assignment over the woman. The spirit left the house, and I turned around to see the woman sitting up and wanting something to eat. Once again evil was pushed back, and God's life was brought forth. The prophetic does have impact.

Conclusions

The impacts of the prophetic voice are widespread, making it one of the most important gifts involved in the fulfillment of God's plan. The greater amount of love, the greater the impact of the prophetic voice. The fears and doubts of God's people have blinded their eyes to the prophetic voice so they do not know what he is doing. In these days, the outpouring of the Spirit is sweeping away those hindrances and letting the prophetic voice be heard loud and clear, so God's plan will prevail. Obedience to the prophetic voice ignites the revival fires so his glory may cover the earth.

Chapter 10
CONCLUSIONS:
BRIDGE TO YOUR LIFE

As my prophetic voice rises and penetrates the earth, my perfect will be accomplished and my kingdom established, says the Lord. Let the earth rejoice and let the heavens proclaim my majesty and my coming.

The prophetic voice is declaring all the great and mighty works of the Lord. His kingdom is always increasing, so the prophetic voice is constantly sounding. It is increasing like a raging fire which cannot be quenched. The Lord can speak thorough anything, but he chooses willing vessels to carry his pure, fiery word. The prophetic voice burns up carnality and brings forth God's will in the lives of people. Are you willing to discover your calling and take up the torch of fire to prophesy and speak prophetically for him?

Developing the Prophetic Gift

The prophetic voice is proclaimed by those who are called to prophesy, intercede, psalm and/or serve as a prophet. The prophetic voice helps people understand God's will and develop a closer relationship with him. It is important for you to find your part in the prophetic voice and fulfill your calling.

PROPHETIC VOICE RISING

Understanding the role of the spirit of the prophet is important for a person with a prophetic gift. The Holy Spirit communes and communicates with a prophet through the spirit of the prophet. The spirit of the prophet has to be nourished, ignited with God's fire and released in order for the prophetic voice to be clearly heard. As the spirit of the prophet develops, it overtakes and crucifies the flesh.

Those with a prophetic gift cannot hide in a religious setting where the prophetic voice is rejected and expect their gift to be unaffected. Doubt and unbelief hinder people from developing their gift. They need to come out from the unbelievers. Relationships with those who resist the prophetic voice and speak against it hinder a person's prophetic gift. Staying with those who reject the prophetic voice destroys a person's confidence in the prophetic gift.

Those with a prophetic gift need spiritual relationships with mature believers who flow with the prophetic. They need to find their spiritual family. It is important for them to be surrounded by prophetic people who challenge and inspire them. They need a support system which includes those who speak prophetically and those who intercede prophetically. They can become involved with the prophetic voice by interceding prophetically for others. The kingdom operates by the principle of sowing and reaping. If you need intercessors begin to intercede for others. Be faithful in another person's ministry, and the Lord will bring forth your ministry.

Activating the Prophetic Ministry

Activating your prophetic ministry begins with seeking the Lord. He will show you his purpose for you through his word and by his Spirit. Find the relationships God has ordained for you, and let those people help prepare you and send you under proper authority. Prophetic authority is delegated authority which comes from being under authority to those with authority. Those who operate prophetically in isolation from the body of Christ are rejected and wounded by others. Their prophetic gifts often operate out of their wounds and bitterness rather than out of love. Spiritual relationships will help protect you and keep you in God's love.

The prophetic voice cannot be contained in the four walls of a traditional congregation. Sound it in the work place, the market place and wherever people need to hear from God. The prophetic voice is needed especially in dark and hard places where people are hurting. The prophetic voice will impact the oppressed in these places and set them free. Those running from the Lord may be found in such places as jails, prisons and drug rehabilitation centers. They have not found the place where they fit into society, because they are looking in the wrong places. They need someone to intervene in their lives. Many in religious institutions are busy with mundane activities without knowing God's purpose for them. The prophetic voice calls them out and directs them towards the Lord and their destiny.

Spreading Revival Fires

The rise of the prophetic voice corresponds to the outpouring of the Holy Spirit. The prophetic voice is preparing the glorious church for Christ's return. Men's efforts apart from the Spirit are divided and limited, so they cannot reach the lost or prepare the church for its destiny. Divisions in the church will never be eliminated through man's efforts. Religious groups, prayer meetings and even revival meetings are not unifying the church. The unity of the Spirit brings the church together. Mass media efforts to reach the lost are inadequate. Multitudes live beyond the reach of technology. The multitudes will be reached one person at a time by men, women, boys and girls who carry God's fiery word. Signs and wonders attract the multitudes, because they express the reality of God's will.

The Spirit's words radiate energy which can be manifested in such ways as creative miracles, light (enlightenment) and fire. Pursue the light of God's knowledge and embrace his power which is being released as energy. The Spirit's life-giving energy brings God's glory into the earth. The prophetic voice contains both the knowledge and power of the Spirit's words to ignite revival fires. Answer God's call and be his prophetic voice to ignite fire in the hearts of people in your family, in your community and every place he sends you.

NOTES

A Request for Your Review

If you enjoyed this book, please review it on Amazon.

A Book on Finances by Fred and Sherry White

Walking in the Father's Riches

Are you facing financial problems? This book is a lifeline for those people seeking the way out of their financial problems. It will help you overcome these problems and walk in the true riches of the heavenly Father.

A Book on Marriage by Fred and Sherry White

Marriage by the Spirit: Rhythms of Grace

Find fulfillment and joy in marriage by following the Holy Spirit's rhythms of grace. This book offers a fresh approach to marriage and relationships. It includes revelation of God's plan for marriage and offers practical strategies to improve your marriage.

Contact Us on the Web

www.FredAndSherryWhite.com

www.ingramcontent.com/pod-product-compliance
Lightning Source LLC
Chambersburg PA
CBHW031326040426